# It's Easy to Be Healthy

## by Toni Castro

## Table of Contents

# Chapter 1
# Get Going

Sitting is easier than being active. It's easier to take the bus than to walk. It's easier to play a computer game than to run on a basketball court.

However, sitting is not good for your body. You need **exercise**. When you sit, your muscles don't have much to do so they get smaller. You aren't as strong. And you get tired faster.

Moving makes you healthier. Doing any kind of activity helps you stay healthier.

Always stretch before exercising. ⤷

The key to exercising well is to be sure to choose something you like to do. Otherwise, you won't want to do it for long.

You don't have to do all of your daily exercise at the same time. You may decide to walk to school. Then take a bike ride after school. That's just as good for you as doing the same amount of exercise all at once.

## A Healthy Stretch

Do some stretches before you exercise. Stretching warms up your muscles before you use them. It gets them ready to work. Plus, it makes you less likely to get hurt.

Exercising may make you feel a little warm. You may be a bit out of breath. That's good. It means you are getting a good workout. It also means your heart is pumping blood to the rest of your body.

Here's a tip. Try to talk while you're doing an activity. If you can, then you're doing the right amount of exercise.

## Too Much TV

How many hours of television do you watch every week? By the time many kids are 18 years old, they will have watched more than 19,000 hours of television. That's more than two years of watching TV around the clock! If people watched less TV, they would have more time to exercise.

So make a plan. Get active. Start slowly. A little exercise is better than none. Work up to what makes you feel healthy and happy.

Riding bikes is a great way to exercise. ↻

# Chapter 2
# Good Eating

Never skip breakfast. That's not a healthy way to start the day. Breakfast is the most important meal of the day. Eating eggs, fruit, cereal, or yogurt will start your day off right. You'll stay awake at school and learn more easily.

Your body needs food to gain energy. Bread, cereals, rice, tortillas, and pasta are all good foods that give you energy.

Your body needs good **nutrition** to grow. Lean meat, chicken, fish, eggs, and dairy products build muscles and bones. Nuts and soy products are good for you, too.

↻ Eating good food keeps you strong and healthy.

Fruits and vegetables have many of the vitamins your body needs. You should have seven servings of fruits and vegetables every day. Vegetables and fruits that have different colors give you different vitamins.

⊙ This food pyramid shows the many kinds of foods you need to eat to stay healthy.

GRAINS | VEGETABLES | FRUITS | MILK | MEAT & BEANS

Foods with a lot of fat, sugar, or salt are not good for you. Too much fat and salt can lead to heart disease and weight gain. Too much sugar can lead to weight gain and tooth **decay**.

In fact, too much of anything isn't good. Eating the right amount of food is a big part of being healthy.

↺ Choose a piece of fruit as a snack.

## Junk Foods

Some people love soda, chips, candy, and cookies. But these foods are made up mostly of sugar and fat. They don't keep your body healthy. These "junk" foods may taste good, but so do a lot of healthier choices.

You also need to drink plenty of water to be healthy. A body needs water even more than food. People can live for many weeks without food. But people can't live without water for more than a few days.

More than half of your body is made up of water. In fact, blood is mostly made from water. But your body loses water all the time. You lose water when you breathe out and when you sweat. Make sure that you drink enough water to stay healthy.

You should drink four to six glasses of water everyday. ⟳

# Chapter 3
## No Germs, Please

Even if you are exercising and eating right, you can still get sick. **Germs** can make you sick.

There are some simple things you can do to get rid of germs. The easiest way is to wash your hands. You should wash your hands after you use the bathroom and before each meal.

↻ Be sure to use soap when you wash your hands.

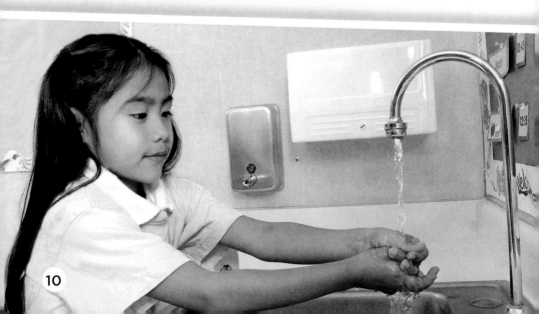

⌒ A bandage
helps keep
your cut clean.

## Cover Your Cut

You are less likely to get a scar if you cover a cut with a bandage. Plus, a bandage can help your cut heal. Some bandages even come with medicine in them.

Take care of your cuts. If the skin is broken, germs can get into your blood. Ask an adult to help you clean the cut. Use an **antiseptic** to kill any germs. Then cover the cut with a bandage. These steps will help the cut heal.

# Chapter 4
# Eyes, Ears, and Teeth

Do you have trouble seeing the chalkboard from the back of the classroom? If so, it's time to get your eyes tested. You shouldn't worry if your doctor informs you that you should get glasses. You may need them for reading or to see far away.

If you have trouble hearing, you should have a hearing test. Some people who have trouble hearing can hear better with a tiny hearing aid in their ear.

Glasses that fit well can even be worn when you play sports. ↻

🎧 Brush your teeth for at least two minutes to be sure they are clean.

Your teeth are another part of your body that you need to care for. After all, they have to last a long time. You need them to chew food. You want to keep your beautiful smile, too.

To keep your teeth healthy, brush them at least twice a day. **Floss** between your teeth, too. You should also get two checkups each year at the dentist. The dentist will tell you how to keep your teeth and gums healthy.

Have you ever heard the saying, "A healthy mind in a healthy body"? Doing everything you can to be healthy is a personal choice. Get serious about your health. If you exercise, eat right, and have all your checkups, you will have a good chance of being healthy and happy.

Always have fun when you exercise.

# Glossary

**antiseptic** *(an-ti-SEP-tik)* something that kills germs *(page 11)*

**decay** *(de-KAY)* a slow, natural breaking down of animal or plant matter *(page 8)*

**exercise** *(EK-suhr-sighz)* activity to improve the body or mind *(page 2)*

**floss** *(FLAWS)* to clean between teeth using a waxed thread *(page 13)*

**germs** *(JURMZ)* tiny living things that can make other living things sick *(page 10)*

**nutrition** *(new-TRISH-uhn)* the process by which food is taken in and used by a living thing *(page 6)*

---

# Index

# Comprehension Check

## Retell

Use the photos to help you retell the information in this book.

## Think and Compare

1. Turn to page 13. What should you do to keep your teeth healthy? In what order should you do these things? *(Identify Sequence of Events)*

2. What are some of the things you do to keep yourself healthy? *(Apply)*

3. What do you think people in charge of schools can do to help their students stay healthy? *(Analyze)*